My Adventure to the National Zoo

Dr. Michaele C. Samuel
Adam G. Ishaeik

My Adventure to the National Zoo is the first book in the Anthology of Chase's Adventures.

ISBN: 10:1530993911

ISBN-13: 978-153099391

To Sabba and Safta, beloved grandparents.

AMERICAN
BISON
zoo

My Adventure to the National Zoo

Hello, I am Chase. I have been learning about animals. I learned about different kinds of animals, their names, what they eat and the sounds that they make.

My parents took me to the National Zoo in Washington, DC to see some of the animals I have been learning about. I was so excited. I grabbed my shoes and ran to the door before my parents were ready to leave.

On the way to the zoo I wanted daddy to drive faster. “Go, go, go,” I said. I was very excited! It was my first visit to the zoo.

When we arrived everything looked so big. Some workers checked my parents' bags then we began the adventure. I was very happy to be at the zoo. I wanted to run around. I wanted to see all of the animals.

Our first stop was to see the sloth bear. It looked like a large, black, stuffed animal with floppy ears.

Then we saw the Asian elephants. They were very big and had dirt all over them. The elephants looked like they needed a warm, sudsy bath. One of the elephants lifted its trunk into the air.

"Elephants have two nostrils in their trunk that they use to breathe. They can also soak up water into their nostrils and then blow it into their mouth," said mommy.

The elephants seemed lazy because they did not move around a lot. They were smelly too! I liked the elephants though. They looked just like the pictures on my word cards.

Next, we saw the Asian small clawed otters. I liked the otters. Sometimes they stood on their hind legs. They moved around as if they were very busy going somewhere.

I was having so much fun. The zoo is a lot of fun. Mommy was taking pictures of all of the animals. Everytime we stopped my parents told me things about the animals.

We went into the small mammal exhibit. It was my least favorite exhibit. It was a little dark and you can smell the different animals. Mommy stopped to look at the banded mongooses. The mongooses moved very fast. They looked like big rats.

Daddy said that banded mongooses live in groups of ten to twenty in their natural *habitat*. *Habitat* is the place where a plant or animal normally lives and grows.

We did not spend a lot of time in the small mammal exhibit.

We leaned over the railing to look at an alligator. It was lying still on the grass. We looked at the alligator for a few minutes. It never moved.

We walked to the Giant Panda exhibit. There were so many people looking at the pandas. It was the most popular animal at the zoo.

giant panda

We stopped at the waterfall. Mommy said that she wished the waterfall were in our backyard.

There were a lot of turtles in the pond. There was a beautiful duck in the water too! Some of the turtles were moving very slowly on a log. I enjoyed watching them.

We headed down the Great American Trails. I was walking ahead of my parents because I was so excited to see the other animals.

“Slow down Chase,” said daddy.

“You’ll get to see all the animals”

AMERICAN
TRAIL
TREASURES OF NORTH AMERICA

We saw many more animals: wolves, seals, beavers, and birds. We saw two bald eagles too! My parents said that the bald eagle is both the national bird and national animal of the United States of America.

The wolves looked like large dogs and they were pacing back and forth. Daddy said that one of the wolves is under the care of a *veterinarian*. A *veterinarian* is a person who takes of care sick or injured animals.

The zebra was far away from where we stood. It had black and white stripes. The zebra looked a little sad and lonely.

The last exhibit we saw was the American bison. They were very big. They had curved, sharp horns and did not look very friendly.

I enjoyed my first adventure to the National Zoo. The zoo is a lot of fun! My parents promised to take me to the San Diego Zoo when we visit our family in California.

I can hardly wait!

www.ingramcontent.com/pod-product-compliance
Lightning Source LLC
Chambersburg PA
CBHW041522280526
45792CB00004B/1346

* 9 7 8 1 5 3 0 9 9 3 9 1 8 *